T0078036

LEAVE, NO STONE UNCOVERED

DANIEL MICHAEL

authorHOUSE®

AuthorHouse™
1663 Liberty Drive
Bloomington, IN 47403
www.authorhouse.com
Phone: 833-262-8899

Published by AuthorHouse 10/20/2020

ISBN: 978-1-7283-7370-6 (sc)
ISBN: 978-1-6655-0167-5 (e)

Library of Congress Control Number: 2020918776

Print information available on the last page.

This book is printed on acid-free paper.

As I put the letter back in the envelope, I sat by the dinner-table trying to recall the past, the past that created my earliest memory

Contents

Acknowlegements ix

Introduction xi

Chapter 1   The Letter 1

Chapter 2   The Heart of Africa (1988) 9

Chapter 3   From Libya to Egypt (1992) 51

Chapter 4   From Egypt to India (1992-2004) 63

Chapter 5   Revisit the heart of Africa 99

Glossary 121

Activities 123

Acknowlegements

I already created places journey in my mind, it was an idea long time ago when I was at high school. I said to myself when I grew up, someday, somewhere, I would demonstrate six stages of Belfour's life.

I very much thank my spouse whom I rely on her whenever I needed support. From here, I dedicated this draft to my spouse, without her support this work would not be achieved.

I would also like to thank my elder daughter whom I keep sharing my perspectives and perceptions in term of demonstrating these six stages. She also had a huge impact on this work, without her support this draft-work would not be possible.

I would also like to dedicate this work to all members of my family, in particular, my three daughters and son, in order to encourage them in their academic career and inspire them to learn something from it and reap perseverance and success.

Introduction

To begin with, not all characters in this book are intended to be based on actual characters, except one, David Belfour, the main character in this book. Not all events in this book are intended to be based on actual events except three. The events that occurred are amongst immigrant families who moved recently to Canada seeking comfort and a better life. Most of the stories in this book are based on actual events in different places at different times. Belfour was a student at Mohall University, Udaipur city, India in 1990. Belfour was studying Bachelor of Arts in English literature.

It is a story of a person who fled from his native land to another place because of oppression.

It is a story of a person who escaped from his native land to another place because of ignorance.

In time, of course, there were hundreds of international students from the heart of Africa studying in the city of Udaipur. It was considered one of the most beautiful cities in India. There are many interesting sights to attract tourists to visit, the places of cultural heritage, such as lakes, palaces, gardens and temples. Therefore, Udaipur is being named The City of Lakes. The city welcomes visitors every day. They come from different countries to explore. The city is vibrant, magnificent and rich in cultural events. Visitors come from their home lands to learn about Indian cultures and folks.

Belfour had also been working in Libya for more than three years. He had been doing two things at the same time. He had been working on a farm in the mornings and planning for his career in the evenings.

Does he know what lies ahead?

In time, the standard of living in Libya for Belfour was not as good as the standard of living in India. There were six important places in Balfour's life. India was one of them Belfour visited. He studied English in India because he wanted to move forward to a community where English is the national language. If Belfour was asked what one place in his life he would like to revisit, it would be India.

Belfour composed the following stanza and kept repeating it all time:

Do not be weak, you've reached the peak

Do not be weak, walk around the creek

Do not be weak, you deserve a treat.

Do not be weak, now sit on the peak.

Belfour was fascinated by the simple life in Libya. He was very courageous with ambition to strive for a better life. In the ninetieth century he made a decision to fly to India. He chose India from amongst many countries to study because India was cheaper.

Chapter 1

THE LETTER

A TALL POST MAN passed by Waterloo University with many letters in his hand. Next to University was a home and he knocked gently on the door.

I stood up from the dinner-table where I was sitting, and said, "Come in".

The post man opened the door, stepping in.

"I have a letter for you from the Waterloo post-office. Management has asked me to hand deliver it to you."

"That was so kind of you, thank you," I spoke.

"Not at all, have a great day," the post man replied.

"You as well," I answered.

Seconds passed. I looked at the letter. It was sealed in an envelope, stamped **Westdeutsche Post, Stadt Gießen**.

I did not know who it was from. The letter was not written in English. I kept turning the letter over and over in my hands many times, but I did not understand the language on the back letter!

I felt nervous! Furious! Sigh!

"What is this language?

"What the heck," I say to myself out of anger; I could not control my emotions.

I was really confused at first about it. I wanted to know whether the letter concerns me or not. While I was thinking about it, the doorbell rang. I opened the door and welcome my neighbor

Mr. Hargreaves who lives next to me. Mr. Hargreaves was a retired University professor. We have known each other for a long period of time, because we both live in Waterloo and we were neighbors for years.

Hargreaves stepped in to invite me for dinner-party next Friday. The dinner-party made for his son's graduation from the University College. The dinner-party was going to take place at a hotel in Kitchener. I accepted the invitation. At the same time, I told him I have just received this letter, but it was not written in English. It was in another language, I did not understand it.

"May I look at it," Hargreaves asked.

"Yes" I answered as I handed him the letter.

"This letter is written in German," Hargreaves expressed!

German, I asked?

"Yes, it is German language, my friend-. I have been to Germany many times & know the language very well," Hargreaves replied.

Then I ask him to who it was from.

    Wolf Muller

    Rabanur Street 10, Giessen

    Germany.

I thanked Hargreaves for his time and inform him I am going to open the letter and try to read it myself. But if I find it in German language, I will ask you for help.

"I must go now." Hargreaves said as he approached the door.

I asked him before he left, how did you learn Germen language?

"I lived in Germany for more than four years with my brother; my brother had already been there for ten years" Hargreaves responded.

Thank you for accepting my dinner invitation. Until then, have a good night my friend.

"You as well, my friend."

I sat in the quiet as I thought about the letter. Before I opened it, I tried to recall the person whose name was on the back of the letter. After ten minutes of meditation, I faced my trepidation and opened it. Thankfully, it was written in English.

I read it silently and cautiously.

House No 8
The Island
25/8/86

Dear Belfour,

I am very sorry I have not written sooner. I have been very busy travelling with my family to Africa. I have not forgotten the Island and Aljazeera, the Island on the river Nile! I enjoyed the time I stayed at your village and your home!

Here in Germany it's just getting summer now, temperature is rising to more than 22C and I can swim in lakes; it is cold in the morning, when I ride my bike to work. I hope you were doing well. I look forward to your response. My dear Belfour: I assure you that were a nice time in your country and on your island!!

Many greetings
Wolf Muller

As I put the letter back in the envelope, I sat by the dinner-table trying to recall the past, the past that created my earliest memory. I really could not remember such a name "Wolf Muller" at present.

I continued sitting by the dinner-table late into the night trying to remember if I had such a friend in the past.

I started questioning myself,

Why did this man send me a letter?

I read it, I understand it, but it seems to me that something is not normal.

I do not remember this man at all. And even his name sounds strange to me, "Wolf Müller".

I live in the city of Kitchener, in the province of Ontario. The city is a little bit becoming more and more attractive and is a growing tremendously and today contains about 242,000 approximately. The city is becoming very busy during school days, because there are a lot of international students come to study at the Universities. The Universities are busy with local and international students. Some students completed their programs leaving for their homes while new other students coming in. The city is very vibrant and magnificent, because it is close to the big city Toronto. People commute between the two cities by bus or carpool. There are a lot of job opportunities for future generations.

Here in Kitchener it's just getting winter now, temperature is decreasing to more than -10C and we cannot take a bath in lakes; it is not warm in the morning, but sometimes it does get warm in the morning.

In Kitchener there are so many enterprises, factories, small scale industries, Malls, shops, restaurants, Starbucks, Tim Horton, just to name a few.

Kitchener is becoming more expensive than before particularly housing rents, because many people move from other cities to relocate in Kitchener where job opportunities is available for them.

The population in Kitchener is also growing rapidly more than ever before. At the same time, Kitchener-municipality is working continuously to help improve the housing conditions where the majority of people live, the municipality is also working continuously to double the amount of housing that is now are available.

Clark said he is deeply aware of the need, and welcome any creative solutions to see more housing built at a cost people can afford. " I understand the challenges [people] face, I understand the frustration that they have, and I am working hard, using every partner that I have-municipal governments, the federal government, the private sector, the public sector and non-profits, anyone with a good idea that will help that young couple that wants to realize the dream of home ownership, that senior, that person who is homeless or at the risk of being homeless, I am using everything at my disposal to try to help them," he said in an interview.

I really like my city Kitchener, and the new job that I got at the University, in the department of languages and literature. I enjoy working & interacting, listening to and supporting students.

I always feel pretty and amazing when I interact with university students, I feel very comfortable and energetic in such a working environment. This working environment help improve mutual respects, friendship and understanding.

But as I have stated earlier, I sometimes get lonely, get bored, I do not like living here by myself. I look forward to bringing my family over. I already talked to my family on moving here. My new job will assist me to take care of them and live a decent life.

Chapter 2

THE HEART OF AFRICA (1988)

I am originally from the heart of Africa, I was born in Aljazeera (an Island) a major town in the region of white Nile.in the heart of Africa. The population of Aljazeera today is estimated to be about 15,000. The main activity in town was growing crops for food. Town's natural resources are good soils, streams, rivers, Blue Nile and White Nile.

People in the Town were working in fields in the mornings, returning homes in the evenings. People in the Town were very contented and happily with their land. They had a very big Mosque in the center of the Town.

The Mosque was very large, maybe was one of the biggest Mosque in the region at time.

Some people run small businesses in the town, they grew vegetables in the valleys and brought them to town- market every day and sold them. They made good profit from that small business, and that business helped people in the town to get what they needed from the vegetable- market.

The town has two separate high schools, one school for boys and the other ones for girls. There was no co-education in town, people were so conservative, and they did not allow boys and girls to study together in one classroom. They believed co-education was against their traditions and customs. But if you go back to today to the same place, you would find a lot of changes; you would see co-education in schools as well.

Sometimes there may not be enough boys to open school, but if the management put boys and girls together the total number of them will be big enough to run school. Recently people become so open to the world outside. The access to all type of net-work created space for positive change in all walks of life.

There was one big hospital for all people in town and small Health Centre for emergency aid. There was also a small police station in charge of keeping order in Town and small courthouse for demonstrating justice.

The rate of the crime in the Town was not so high, because the vast majority of people know one another and above that they always help one another in terms of food and shelter. Most of the people in Town were very generous and supportive; this type of activities helped reduced the rate of the crime in Town.

I come from a big family; I lived with my parents, I had four brothers and four sisters. We all lived in small house on the river Nile, about one mile from the center of the town. My father was a farmer and was breeding camels on farm. He was a leader in the community, while my mother was a housewife, taking care of home affairs.

She died at the age of fifty
That was sad news for the whole family.
We still remember her and she is still alive in our hearts & minds.

As a young boy, at high school, I was influenced by the social activities of the community in the town,

Figure 1. A photo of the School in the Island, White Nile Province. September 25, 2001.

I continue to be impressed and amazed by the social activities just as festivals related to receive visits, a wedding, death, a birth or someone returns home from a long journey. Those sorts of social activities were managed by a service committee. That service committee was in charge of all social activities and its methodology. Each program was based on the number of the participants. I was a member of that service committee. We actively engaged, helped and organize activities in town.

I was also joined the English society at our school and became an active member in it; I participated in several meetings. My English was not good at that time, but our English teacher was encouraging us to speak English in all meetings. All meetings were related to the importance of learning English as a second language. The rule of the English society enforced all members to speak in English in all meetings. Of course, we made mistakes but we learned from our mistakes.

ANNOUNCEMENT FOR THE FIRST MEETING

DEBATES

MOVIES!   Stories!

JOIN

THE ENGLISH SOCIETY

A meeting of all those interested in beginning an English Society in our high School will be held on Friday September 8th at 7 pm in the Conference Room Number 7

PLEASE JOIN!

HELP TO MAKE OUR SCHOOL MORE INTERESTING.

The above advertisement posted in many classes last week, and about twenty five students participated in the meeting.

Mr. Maki and another English teacher were also there. One student was sitting next to me whispered to his classmate, "Do you think there are enough participants?

Monzer, a shy student, responded, "Oh yes, I think so, twenty five is quite good!"

Mike stood up to address the meeting:

We called you for this meeting to discuss the formation of an English society at our school. I think some of you have been talking about it for long time and I think now is the right time to start it. You know, we do not have cultural activities in our school, if we start one, maybe other activities will follow.

I talked to many students since last week about the perception of starting an English society and found that so many of you are interested in it. Please join us and assist to improve your school activities. Mr. Ibrahim and I are here to help and guide you to make your English society more enjoyable and interesting.

You need time to listen more English and practice it more, so I think it is time to start now. Then you will have an opportunity to practice English speaking skills.

All students applauded Mr. Mike when he sat down. Then a discussion followed. One student suggested speaks English Café, another wanted movies and a third asked for meeting foreigners. By the end of the meeting we had chosen Mr. Mike as the head English, Belfour as a president and Ibrahim as staff advisor.

DURING THE LONG HOLIDAY, I went by the ferry from Aljazeera to Kosti on the river Nile opposite to visit my relative there. In down-town, I met with a foreigner, who came to the city as a tourist, and a conversation followed:

It seems to be a little bit hot; shall we go to that small café to drink something?

That is a good idea," the foreigner said.

"What do you think of this city?

"It looks good and people are nice too," the foreigner answered.

"The city is growing and the municipality and the city have added some new bus services,"

"I would prefer to live in the countryside rather than a city," the foreigner replied.

I would love to live in town, because living in town is more progressive that villages, I said"

"Well, I like countryside life because it is quiet, fresh air and even you know everyone who lives there," the foreigner replied.

"I felt like really enjoy practicing English while talking to you,"

"Your English is good; you should visit western modern countries for more practice,"

Oh, that was the bus I came on, I want to catch it now to go back to my room to have a nap, the foreigners said. Adding I thank you very much for your invitation and I hope we meet again.

"So sorry, I did not ask you about your name," I asked.

Oh, my name is Muller, from German,

Thank you, good bye and have a good evening.

A week later, I went to down-town to find someone new to talk to, but I did not find any one there so I went to catch the bus to go back home. As I was waiting for the bus, I saw Muller whom I met last time. He was walking and looked very sad. I immediately ran to him and reminded him about the café shop where we met last time and asked him what happened.

He told me that someone stole his wallet and money and now he had nothing.

He wanted to speak to his family and ask them to send him money. I told him not to worry, that I will help you out to get some money now, I went to the high school in Kosti and told the principal about the event and he was very pleased to help. The principal told me to bring him to school tomorrow after breakfast.

The principal had already asked students to bring donation from their homes to help out the foreigner who has been stolen or lost his money. And all students informed their parents and brought their donation.

Next morning Muller and I went to the school and met the principal in his office. He was very happy to meet Muller and told him he had received news that Muller had been robbed and informed him we now had good news for him.

We collected nearly one thousand dollars. Muller was very happy and thankful to all of us.

The principal suggested we needed to do more to help others who are in need sometimes, to reflect our values and generosity because we never know when it might happen to one of us.

I never heard about Muller since that time, he may be left for his country or he went to another place to visit, he had been given enough money to help him to settle down for a while and be in touch with his family back home, we were very happy to help.

The high school was beautifully located in a quiet area near the river Nile, about three miles from the center of the town. Mr. Ibrahim was the principal of the high school for boys. He was always encouraging people in town to send their children to school. By that time, the school had two English teachers. One had arrived from England. His name was Mr. Mike. The other was a Sudanese English teacher, his name was Mr. Maki. Mr. Maki had studied English in England and knew it very well. He has recently become the head of the English society.

Mr. Maki held many seminars in English at the high school. Most of his meetings address the following questions:

- How we learn English?
- What English we learn?

Mr. Maki responded to above questions persuasively. He had delivered all his seminars in the conference room at the high school. I actually listened attentively to Mr. Maki while he was lecturing the audience .And even I was impressed by his incredible comments on students' questions.

Students walk three miles to get to school in the mornings and return home in the evenings. They loved their school days, but they did not like reading and writing. At school, they liked spending most of their time playing games with one another. The majority of them come from poor families. They do not have enough food to eat. Most of them come to school with empty stomach.

There is now a school cafeteria program. The school cafeteria program is run by the school administration. It feeds the students one affordable meal per day. The school lets them get a drink of water from a tap that runs from the river Nile. The water is safe according to the Town's health standards.

During the break, you could see students gathering around the tap like birds to a birdbath. Students were drinking lots of water to fill themselves up before they left school. Each one of them was waiting for his turn.

We sometimes have social activities in the school, such as Football, volley ball and race. Some of my classmates would prefer to go swimming in the River Nile. The majority of my classmates know how to swim, but the principal of the school does not allow them to go swimming.

My favorite game was a football; I used to play a goal keeper. I was very professional goal keeper. I used to play a goal keeper for a small team in the school. The name of the team was Al-hilal. Our team participated in different football match in the Island. We won in many matches against other teams in other schools.

I had a very close friend in the class, his name is Bashir, and we usually spend much time together after school days. He was very smart in school, he knows math very well. Everyone in the school understands that Bashir was the best student in math at our school.

Someday he went to swim in the River Nile by himself. He knows that I do not like swimming in the River Nile, he does not tell me that he wants to go to swim. He took his small bag pack and went to the river.

It was very windy day and you can see few small boats on the river, because of the bad weather. Many fishers stop fishing on that windy day, but Bashir does not understand that swimming in the windy day was dangerous. He started swimming in the river and the wind blows very strongly.

You can see waves rolling behind waves, big waves and sometimes small waves. Bashir knows how to swim but while he was swimming against the current, the big waves covered him, and he could not resist the big waves. During that time, there was one fisher was walking on the bank of the river for fun. He saw Bashir went down the river for a while and could not be able to show up. He knew that Bashir was in terrible, he needs help, the fisherman jumped into the water and swam very rapidly toward Bashir, but he did not find him.

He started searching in the area where he saw Bashir for long time but he did not see him. He spent more than half an hour in the water searching for Bashir. Unfortunately Bashir had drawn into the river and died. It was very sad news to the school and the Island.

I was shocked when I received the bad news, since that day, the school issued a tough rules for all students never go swimming in the river during the whole week. And also the community in the Island warned all students and forbid swimming in the river.

Before that event took place, the school allows students to go swimming under the supervision of a captain, but after the death of Bashir, the program of swimming has been cancelled forever.

I still remember my friend Bashir; I still remember his shadow that never goes away from me. I kept myself busy to avoid thinking about him, but it was becoming very hard and uneasy to forget such a nice friend, he is still lives and kicking in my hearts. The only thing that I can do to please him is to pray for him.

The good thing that, I will never forget it in my life is bond of the community in the Island. One such example, the high school does not have border to accommodate the new students who come from other villages.

The community in the Island has a nice social program for the new students. The community committee approaches the school and distributes all the new numbers of students in the community. Each family has to host one or two students for the whole program. The new student live with a family as a member family, the family truly treated him as one of the member of the family.

on weekends the Community organizes short trips for students to Tayba garden. The goal of the trip was to keep students busy and happy at the same time.

Figure 2. A photo of Tyba Garden, White Nile Province. September 25, 2001.

Tayba garden is located on the river Nile. It is about seven miles from the school. Students usually go to tayba garden by bus. They go in the morning and return in the evening. The garden was very rich with all kinds of fruits.

In 1985, the community organized one picnic for all students at our school to Tayba garden. I could not remember how old would I have been at that time, but I still remember I was in that picnic. There was one thing that had drawn my attention while I had been visiting

23

Tayba garden. I saw different types of flowers and trees along the road that runs from down-town to Tayba garden.

The bus was moving on a wide road, surrounded by shaded trees from both sides. The shady trees have blocked the sun's rays from the bus that runs under the shades of the trees while it had been heading to Tyaba garden.

It was a damp morning, I could not be able to see the sun because of the foggy weather and rich trees grow on both sides of the road.

It was very wonderful scenery. In the garden I met with more than twenty employees. Their work was to help the visitors to get in and have fun.

It was free for all students to get in the garden and eat any type of fruits. There were aloft of mangos, guavas, grapefruits, bananas, grapes just to name few.

When I entered the thick garden, I felt as I was in a real paradise. The breeze blows freshly and coolly. I sat under a big tree and started eating some frutis. The gardener keeps feeding me with all types of fruits.

I did not have to pay a single Penney, the only thing I could do was to take my trash away and leave the garden clean. Then I went out of the garden and found myself in small cafeteria where so many people were sitting and yapping with one another. I sat by small table and ordered a cup of tea. It was afternoon and the weather was very moderate.

I enjoyed that short trip with my classmates to the garden, and some of my classmates spent much of their time inside the garden, eating and playing hide and seek.

I liked to be by myself to enjoy the delicious moments in different places. I visited different areas inside and outside the garden. I saw some people waiting for the ferry to cross the river to Tayba shore to take them to the opposite side of the river.

I saw a group of people were sitting in small coffee shop. Most of them were foreigners. I went and joined them. They were sitting around a big table that full of traditional portrait coffee cups.

I looked at the traditional portrait on the table and I understood that the coffee table demonstrated friendship, respects and peace in mind. I talked to the group and I got to know that they all had come from different countries.

They did communicate in English and I was lucky to be able to communicate with them in English. Some of them came from Europe and some from Australia. They did have different accent in spoken English but they all spoke fluently.

I spent half an hour with them and I got to know that they all were foreigners. They came to visit the heart of

Africa and learn about African culture. They read a lot about Africa in general before they came to visit it.

They had already spent a week in kosti town and they would plan to visit many places in Africa. I helped them to learn about the beautiful places in Africa and how did they go to see them.

One of the groups was a writer in Australia. He told me that when he returns home, he would write a book about the Sudanese traditional coffee shop. I was thinking how he was going to write a book about this small photo of the Sudanese traditional coffee cups.

I was so excited and amazed by his perspective that he was going to write a book from small coffee shops in Sudan.

Today the time has come and made me thought to write a book related to my person travel experience around the globe. It was not uneasy to write from the very beginning, but with determination and inspiration I would be able to gather all my thoughts and put it into order. I excited to see all my dreams had become true.

The visitors asked me to accompany them to some interesting places as a tourist guide, but at that time, I was student and I apologized! I got their names and address in Kosti. I promised to visit them in Kosti before they leave for some other places across the country.

I saw many people, men, women, boys and girls come to the garden to buy some fruits and spend good time in the thick garden. That kind of short trip in Tayba garden helps to attract students from other villages near the Island also to come to study at the high school.

That type of social interaction was very moving and touching. I remembered the Island was hosting students from different cultural background, but they are all living together in peace and harmony.

Later, I learned better English vocabulary from Mr. Maki. I got courageous and delivered a presentation entitled "Learning English Becomes a Necessity". Everybody in the conference room applauded me when I sat down. The applause of the audience inspired me to step out and responded to audience' questions.

I made a lot of friends at school and outside of school. Later I was elected as the head of the English society, and Mr. Mike was elected as staff advisor. I felt I did not want to be in Aljazeera any longer. I wanted to leave for another country; and even my friends in town felt the same; they felt that I was going to leave them soon. I told them that their feelings impacted on my heart deeply. Mr. Mike advised me to visit England for a while to practice English skills. I replied with a smile. I said, I would love to visit England, but to achieve this goal, it requires a lot of expenses and it might not be affordable.

I kept myself busy at meeting with foreigners whom I met in town, we enjoyed the time we spent together, and learned from one another. We had good time by visiting speakers including other foreigners. The time I spent with others not only improved my English abilities but also had become a turning point in my life.

From 1989 up to December 2019, the situation in the heart of Africa has been declining socially, culturally and economically. Let me give you a brief on all those three aspects of life.

During that tenure, the country was ruling by a dictator who imposed the social discrimination in all communities. He concentrated on creating problems among tribes to divide and rule. He neglected all small minorities in all parts of the country.

For instance, if you want to apply for a job, you have to fill out a form that discloses your tribe. If you belong to a small tribe that does not have influence in the community, you will not get a job. If you were against the regime, you would be declined a job as well.

Culturally, a vast number of people have ignored their cultural value when it comes to the matter of help and supporting elders in public transportation. Nowadays very few young people respect elders in terms of help. Many youths are only thinking of themselves. For example, if an older man gets onto the bus, no one cares to stand up and let him be seated, but before that era, people help and support elders in every place and at any time of the day.

Economically the country fell in huge debt and all people are suffering from the financial crunch. All businesses now seemed to be in the hand of the dictator. The rest of the population continues to suffering from this policy. The majority of people weren't able to put food on the table.

Weather condition

It was the beginning of fall season, there was very little rain, and there were few clouds in the sky. The sun was a little bit warm and the weather condition was moderate. The farmers started talking about the shortfall of rain. There sometimes were dark clouds in the sky. Farmers were expecting heavy rain, but there was no rain all year round. The sky looked clear. The cultivation of land was not done yet for the crops.

The blue birds and green birds do not fly over the fields anymore. All fields withered and died. The ghost of hunger came down near the city borders. The children were afraid of being sick and ignore. The parents were afraid of being unhappy eyes never sleep at nights.

Omer was a preacher in the big Mosque. He usually led prayers at the Mosque in town where most attended. So he asked his congregation to pray for rain. Men, women and children all prayed. There was no rain. Maybe the Lord didn't hear their prayers.

Figure 3. A photo of AlKon Mosque, White Nile Province. September 25, 2001.

Farmers were very aware of the dangers they were going to face in the absence of rain. They were going to face drought. The drought meant lots of people would go hungry, and the people would face crisis of food and water insecurity. Farmers were struggling to keep their animals and families while their silos food consumed.

As youth were leaving their town for another place, animals were also leaving for another place seeking for pasture and water.

The preacher gathered all his people in the Mosque and spoke "the town is a place where we were born to live". Indicating that he wanted all people to stay with him in the island and face whatever was going to occur. People had decided to stay with the preacher and face challenges. Animals were suffering from the lack of grass. The cracked valleys do not hold water any more. Rivers were drying up and animals were dying.

It was hard for people to maintain the broken land, and dry rivers.

It was hard for people to feed their children and maintain animals

It was hard for everyone to survive.

They wanted find to a better place.

Under these circumstances, I spoke out in public about the idea of moving from the town to another place but people in town disapproved and opposed the idea.

I went and talked to my parents about the substantial situation in town, and how much people of town are going to suffer. My parents had already known about the difficult time and they were not going to listen to me. My father just uttered, "You are right, my son, the life was becoming very difficult." and we lost all our sheep because the valleys did not hold pasture any more. However, your mother and I had no intention to leave for another place; he added "the town is a place where we were born to live".

Belfour left home (1989)

It was winter time; it was very gloomy and chilly night, the moon had still not yet appeared in the sky. Few stars here and there in the sky, visible to see from a far distance, speckled here and there. I woke up at midnight, while everybody was home in a deep sleep. I packed my bag pack and left home for the last time.

Figure 4. A photo of the road leads to the Island, White Nile Province. September 25, 2001.

I left the home walking down the road. I did not know where I was going. I came out of the town climbing up and down mountain ranges. I kept on walking and walking all day long till I came to a small cave on top of the hill. The sun was setting behind the mountain ranges when I came to the cave. I was very very tired and wore no shoes. The land was rough and coarse. My feet were bleeding because the rocks cut under them. I reached to the cave and knocked on the gate, an old man dressed in rags came out. He was tall and big. He was a magician. His name was Fairy. He was ninety years old, but he looked to be forty. He looks smart. There was fear in my eyes. Fairy welcomed me and let me in. The cave was very big and beautifully decorated with green lights. The cave had everything that I needed. I saw a big table with a large book and lamp on it. Fairy brought me some food and water. I was very hungry. I ate up all food and drank up all water.

Fairy called his servant to check on my feet and clean up the wounds. The servant name was Rubella. Rubella cleaned up the swelling wounds under my feet, and when Fairy touched my feet all my pains were gone. I was very surprised by what Fairy had done and I asked him how he healed my feet.

"I used my power," Fairy replied with smile.

I actually came to know that Fairy was a magician; he knew that I came from the town about ten miles away from the cave. I asked if I could take a nap as I was tired from my long journey. Fairy touched stone in the corner of the cave and within seconds I found myself on a queen bed with soft yellow blanket.

I immediately fell asleep for the rest of the day. At the end of the day, I woke up and found myself alone in the cave. I did not know what to do. While I was wondering where Fairy has gone, I saw a ton of food on the table. I ate some food and drank some fruit juice. I was wondering from where Fairy got all those types of food and fruit?

And how did Fairy live alone in such a big cave?

While I was exploring my surroundings, Fairy came in with three other men and a woman. They all greeted me and disappeared. I asked Fairy where he had been and where the three men and woman had gone.

Fairy responded, "do not be afraid of me, I am a magician, I have been living here for more than seventy years and no one knows, you are the only one that I liked and I appeared to help you". I see people, but people do not see me. I live with my family and friends in the cave." We are about three hundred magicians in this cave. If you want to live with us, I will help you to stay here but you might be scared of some of my friends and family members when you see them in real life situation.

Some of my friends look like human beings but their feet look like a horse's feet, some their hands look like cow's feet, and some have a cat's tail and some do not. But they are very friendly, they all know that you are here with us but no one would dare to harm you. I am the community leader. You are in safe hands; I do not encourage you to stay here more than five days. After five days we would have a Christmas party and all of them would come inside the cave and that might not be safe for you.

I would be happy to assist if you like. I was very grateful to Fairy for the overwhelming generosity that I received from him. Then I told him that I wanted to go to a city where I could go to school.

I loved being engaged in and part of the community. I also loved being helped by the community.

I did not know how far the city was but Fairy told me that it was about hundred miles from the cave. Fairy gifted me a little stone; telling me this stone is valuable. Keep it safe, and tell no body about it. Take it with you wherever you go.

"It is a precious stone" Fairy exclaimed!

This stone brings you happiness and success on condition that you tell no one about it. If you tell about it, your life will be miserable. I was very excited and vowed to keep it as a secret, and tell no body about it.

"Is it time for you to leave now," Fairy insisted.

"Yes it is time to leave for the city we talked about," I said.

Fairy ordered one of his invisible servants to come before me.

The invisible servant showed himself before me and said "My name is Lucky".

. Lucky appeared a perfectly abnormal creature, he looks like a human being, but he has two big wings and saddle on his back.

Fairy ordered Lucky to fly me near the gate of the city. The city name was Jalo. He added "within few minutes Mr. Lucky would put you in front of the main gate of Jalo city.

Fairy put me on the saddle and fastened the belt.

I thanked Fairy for all his supports.

While Lucky flew up –up— and up-- high into the sky, I was enjoying that lovely flight. I was never getting scared of that situation. As Lucky flew high in the air, I enjoyed touching the mist with my hands. I was courageously enjoying it, as if it was lovely game, and even if it was dangerous.

Lucky announced that we are now commencing our descent to the main gate of Jalo city. Lucky landed gently landing on the ground and I got off the saddle and he disappeared. I was left alone near the gate of Jalo.

From the heart of Africa to Libya (1989-92)

It was sunset; the security border was in a deep sleep, I slowly crossed the border without entry visa. I did not know where to go? I kept walking up and down the valleys. The sun was going behind the valleys. I really felt hungry. I had nothing to eat or drink. I fed up with walking; while I was walking my feet plunged into a cliff. From there, I looked down on the valleys and suddenly my eyes fell in small town. My eyes fell in glittering light in the town. I was very excited and amazed by the beauty of the town. I walked for few minutes and I stepped in down-town. I was really hungry. I was looking for a restaurant to get food. The down town was not so busy at the time of sunset, I noticed few people visit shops and walk about. While I kept on searching for a restaurant, I glanced a big sign says "enjoy delicious food". I went into the restaurant and found some African group sitting by a big dinner table talking to one another. To be honest, I did not know what they were talking about; maybe they were talking about their families' social life back home. They all spoke loudly and interrupted one another in conversation.

I was thrilled to perceive such a vibrant community in that restaurant. I sat by one of the dinner table waiting for services. While I was waiting for services, one member of the African group approached and said "hey brotha, come join us." I was so pleased that the invitation come from the African group themselves, and within no time a gigantic meal placed on the diner-table, meat, fish, chicken, rice, and soup. Just to name a few.

At the end of the meal, one old man stepped in and declared to the restaurant owner, "I am looking for someone to work for me". I have a small convenience store and I need an honest young man to take care of it. I have also offer a place for the employee to live.

"I am interested in working for you." I raised my hand and voiced.

The old man and I left the restaurant for the new place. We walked for few minutes and the old man's son showed up by small car and we both got in. It did not take us more than ten minutes to arrive at the new place. The home was not so far from the center of the town. It was a big home, full of furniture. It was neat and tidy.

"This is your new place to live, tomorrow morning my son will come to take you to our new store. He will tell you how much you get, and how many hours you will work," the old man explained.

Next morning, the old man and his son showed up with breakfast, tea, coffee and some dates as well. Then we all drove down-town where their convenience store was located. I worked from nine in the morning to six in the evening. The store sells all sorts of clothes related to men and women. The store was always busy with customers. The store made a lot of money and the owner of the store was very pleased. Within two years the owner of the store had made a decent amount of money.

Someday I informed the owner of the store" I have a dream and I needed to fulfill my dream".

"What did you say," the owner asked.

"The happiest days in my life, when I see myself joining a college or a university and going from lecture to lecture gaining knowledge," I answered.

"I will increase your salary and benefit, please never quit the job, I trust you and I do not want you to leave the job," the owner muttered.

After three years of work experience have passed with the store, I told the owner I wanted to leave the town to explore another place. The owner was opposing and refusing my resignation, I kept convincing him on leaving the job for Tripoli the capital of Libya seeking a better offer.

"The stone I got it from the magician was in my pocket all time. The stone kept me so strong that I never thought about something else. I was always thinking about my stone and attempting to keep it as a secret," I said.

In Tripoli, I found the majority of inhabitants were not contented with their standard of living. To me their standard of living was okay, except when it comes to human rights pertaining freedom of thought, and expression. All those human values were deprived from them in the name of power. The ruler was all in all, the whole authoritative power in his hand. The ruler did not respect his people, he always treated them badly; he had a big army and a big prison. He opened a big prison to silence the voices of those who demanded rights in public or speak out for justice.

At the time, I was eyewitness to the abuse of human rights in Tripoli. "The town looked like a big prison with little comfort. My ambition was beyond that, my ambition was the stone I got from the old man in the cave. I did not want to lose it or misplace it in unknown zone. I wanted to make sure that I got it right and invested it right," as I promised.

I approached different missions in Tripoli to try to get an entry visa to Europe. But I was not able to get it. Eventually, I rented small car from Tripoli to drop me in Jalo, a town located in the South of Libya. The trip took five hours by car to get there. I remembered the name of the taxi driver, his name was Sahel. He was so nice and kind to me. The trip was so long then we had a nice social chat together.

The taxi driver started asking me several questions:

- Where did you come from?

"I came from the heart of Africa, from Sudan, the biggest country in Africa," I said.

- How old are you?
- I- I- I'm twenty … five years old.
- What? How old are you?
- Twenty five years old.
- "Do you have some relatives in the place where you go now"?
- I felt uncomfortable with some of his questions, but I said, Oh, yes, my brother lives and works there.

"Oh that is cool. I thought you do not have someone there and I was wondering how would you travel alone and you looked so young," The taxi driver commented. He added. 'Last year five young men had been kidnapped by small gang from that place,"

- Which place you were talking about" I asked.

- "Tripoli is a place where different crimes happened and the police weren't able to stop them from happening," the taxi driver said.

After long conversation, I requested him to drop me at that restaurant on the right side of the main road where my brother would come and pick me; I got off the car at the restaurant. The taxi driver gave me his phone number if I needed him again for services, and drove away.

I received a bad news from back home that an elected democratically government was overthrown by the military coup. I really was shocked by that disturbing news. Too see a dictator took over and arrested vast number of civilians and killed civilians in different parts of the country,

The dictator imposed policy that destroyed the educational system and economical system and social system. The majority of youth wanted to leave the country and never thought to come back. The standard of living had become miserable. The beauty of life in the country had totally collapsed. The price of food goes up high in the sky and it might not be affordable. The majority of people in the country could not afford their food on tables.

I continued clinging onto my stone rather than to give up and go back home. During my tenure in Libya, I visited different towns and found out all citizens who live there had the same problems. They were of trepidation and oppression.

I had no connection with my family for a long time and I worried about their lives. I did not know how I could help them. As I was sitting at the Arab cafeteria in down-town, a short Libyan inspector stepped in and asked the customer-service to help him find a person to work in his palm farm.

"I could do that work for you. When do you like me to start? I asked.

The Inspector said, you could start tomorrow if you like, because now it is almost afternoon and the weather seems to be hot. I would take you to the farm to show you how to do the work tomorrow.

"He was a kind man, he had a new car. We both got into the car and drove a short distance before were there. He had a big palace surrounded by a big palm trees. It was not so far from the center of the town," I explained.

"My job was to collect all branches and leaves of the trees and pile up them in one place," The inspector informed. He added "My job was a Captain in the air force; I was in the air force for a while and came home,"

The inspector introduced his father to me, his father name was Jibreal. At the end of the day

I thank them all and went to down town to look for a shelter. I did not tell them I had no place to stay. I went to small lodging in down-town and slept for the night. Next day morning I went to the farm and started working hard to collect all the leaves and branches in one place.

The Inspector thought it would take three days of work for me to clean up the place. But, I had it all done in two days. He was very impressed.

Jibreal informed me "his son is still at work, but he would pay me for the job, he immediately handed me an envelope full of money. I did not count it and I did not know how much was in it. I thanked Mr. Jibreal and was about to leave when Jibreal stopped me" and said "would you please come tomorrow at noon for dinner with us?

We have something to say in the presence of my son," Jibreal said. I accepted the invitation from Jibreal for tomorrow at noon. I returned to my small room in the lodging and asked the waiter to help me count the money! I put the whole amount on the table and requested the waiter to count it for me.

"This is a Dinar currency. One dinar equals three dollars, this is one thousand dinar, if you convert this amount into dollars, and it would become three thousand dollars, wow! That was too much," the waiter said.

In time, I remembered the invitation for dinner and I went on time and knocked the door, the young boy opened the door for me. The boy welcomed me. His age nearly was about twenty years old. I went in and found all the family was waiting in the dining room.

The Inspector introduced me to his parents, sister and wife. The father of the family said let us start eating now maybe Belfour is hungry, we all went to the dining room where I saw a lot of food on the dining-table, they all started eating some meat and macaroni which was considered one of the most delicious and popular food in Libya for Libyans.

While we were busy at enjoying food, the father told me that they have small Farm about two miles from the town. They were looking for someone to live on the Farm and take care of it for a while, the Farm does have a small room for the employee, but it has everything. The employee's job was to water the palms trees. At that moment, I had no other choice. I agreed to live on the farm and attend to the palm trees.

The Farm was located in a desert area, the palm trees usually grow in that environmental area. They took me to that Farm and trained me how to do the job. I lived in that place for a year watering the palm trees and cutting weeds. I learned to be more patient person than ever and to be a strong person in the exile. From time to time, the inspector visited me in the Farm and we together spent good time talk about the difference between food in Libya and Africa.

One evening, the whole family was sitting on the Farm socializing with one another: I took the opportunity to inform them

- — "I decided to fly to India,"
- — "Why would you fly to India,"? The Inspector said.
- — "For educational purposes,"
- — "I have been to Europe several times to take some technical courses, but I do not know why you selected India?" The Inspector said.
- — "Indian people speak English widely and India was cheaper, I would love to go there to study and grasp Basic English skills and later, I would be in a position to utilize that English to explore other countries as well," I explained.
- — "I had good connections with the ministry of education in Tripoli, if you would like to study at the university in Tripoli, I could help you for the admission," The inspector voiced.

–   "I do not want further studies in Arabic countries, thank you for the offer,"

One evening, I was sitting alone in the cafeteria sipping a small cup of tea, an Indian physician came in. he was in white uniform. He sat by the tea- table next to me. He ordered a cup of coffee and small piece of Muffin. He immediately introduced himself to me that he was an Indian physician, his name was Singh Gupta, but now he lives and works in Libya. He went further and asked me what have you been doing in this country? At that moment, I was not yet ready to answer. Then again, he repeatedly asked

"What is your academic qualification?

He added," if you would like to do further studies, I would be more than happy to help you to study in my country. In my country the studies in most universities are in English and the cost of living is cheaper. Adding, the Indian people are very friendly," Singh Gupta said.

"My dream is to study in India and then move to the western countries, but I do not know how to get there," I said. Gupta gave me his contact number and the Hospital where he was working.

A week later, I revisited Gupta in the hospital, I found out that he was a child specialist; he received me with warm hospitality and guided me to submit a copy of my high school certification, because Gupta was flying to in India on vacation.

From there, he would send me an offer of admission form from a college or university. I ran to my room and got my document and right back to him in the hospital.

Within two weeks, I received a call from him saying that my admission letter being faxed to the Indian Embassy in Cairo, Egypt. I was so excited to go to Indian embassy in Cairo to submit my passport for entry visa.

Chapter 3

FROM LIBYA TO EGYPT (1992)

I travelled by taxi from Libya to Cairo. The journey took about six hours. I arrived in Cairo about four in the morning; I heard the voice of Azan from different places calling for prayers. Cairo looked like a bright and wonderful city at dawn. The traffic was a bit slowed down but still you can see billowing smoke gushing from chimneys slowly polluting the fresh air.

I was thrilled to watch Cairo in the morning; the taxi driver dropped me in Opera hotel in the center of Cairo. The streets were full of cars in the morning. The sidewalks were also full of pedestrians, some going to work and some returning home. It took me long time to cross the road, because of numerous vehicles. I had to be very careful when I decided to cross the road or use the intersections.

The city was very busy with a myriad of buses and small cars on streets. I could smell the gas on the streets but I did not know at that time Cairo was so polluted.

I went to bed for a nap and woke up to visit the Indian Embassy for the visa. I remembered at ten o'clock in the morning I met the consul in his office an introduced myself to him. He was very supportive, he looked at my passport and said "we received an offer of admission from Delhi University in your name but we need some time to verify your admission and get back to you

"How long would it take to do so," I inquired.

"Less than a month I would get right back to you," Consul responded.

I really like the life style in Cairo, I was happy to wait for this visa. I went to find other things to do during that time, I also visited some universities in Cairo but I was not interested in studying, my plan was bigger. I learned some Egyptian dialects and made some friends. One day, while I was sitting in a restaurant for breakfast, I received a call from the Indian Embassy in Cairo to submit my passport for student visa.

I was so thrilled that things seem to be worked out so well for me. I rushed to the Embassy, it was an afternoon, and most roads in Cairo were so busy with traffic, small cars, big cars, motor cycles and so many.

I reached the embassy before lunch time and submitted my passport and left, I spent a lot of time in Cairo. They were very lovely days in my life.

I stayed in Cairo for more than a month. I wondered how so many people could live in Cairo. People everywhere in Cairo were so nice and funny too. They love jokes and laugh in a humorous way all the time. That type of social life drew my attention to love Cairo community. Cairo was a beautiful place to visit; I visited so many beautiful places and made so many friends.

The food was very cheap and I liked it, particularly falafel and foul. I liked the bread too. The bread tested very sour but I liked it. I went to Alexandria which is on the Mediterranean Sea. I went to the sea shore and enjoyed the fresh air. I spent a lot of time there. While I was sitting and watching waves rolling behind waves, my thought took me beyond that scenery. I had a very special moment while I was there. I saw many people come to the sea shore. The place was very vibrant and splendid. I went to one of the good universities in Alexandria to see how the educational system works. I found that the educational system at the university was in Arabic and that discouraged me from thinking about continuing it more.

I attended many lectures at the university, but all of them were in Arabic. Most of them talked about the role of education in raising awareness among people, respect and sustainable work that could lead to better economy. Having better economy could lead to a better future for all walks of life.

I enjoyed learning all those topics and lectures but I did not want to do further studies in Arabic. I was looking toward the future and visiting another better place where I can learn, develop and collaborate with other working professional.

In time, Cairo was a place where you could find writers, scholars, poets and on and on, but most of the time those who spoke out for rights of others had problems in terms of freedom of right of expression, some writers believed to be moderate when they wrote and reported issues related to political factors, some writers left Cairo for a place where they could feel free to write. During my stay in Cairo, I came to know the writers' pen is confined and controlled by the ruler of the country. I came to learn from educators Cairo was a rich city in various things.

The life style in the city was full of fun and jokes, the television station and radio station focused on funny stories, story tellers, comedies, music and short report about political event in and out the country. The ordinary people busy working on day to day life. In general, life was looking good, but if you took a closer look, you would see life was not looking good in every way.

One evening, I visited the night club and met with an old man who told me that he used to work for the night club as a gate keeper. We both took a corner table in the club and started talking to each other about different sort of things. One of the most important thing that I had learned from the gate keeper, "so many people kept under the ground for no reasons, so many people lost their jobs for no reasons, so many people were killed for no reasons, and so many people were arrested and tortured for no reasons." The gate keeper said.

The gate keeper also told me that there were many Sudanese people live in Cairo. Most of them fled from their own land owing to poverty and oppression.

They arrived in Egypt and now Most of them live in poor areas around Cairo city, because the rent of most houses around Cairo is cheaper. Some of them get job at small scale industries to put some food on the table.

I learned from the gate keeper a very painful story that happened to one of Sudanese activist in Cairo. His name was Sushi; he used to speak in public and criticized the Sudanese government in Egyptian media press. Someday evening, while he was in his living room in Cairo, the security guard knocked his door and expelled him to Sudan.

What has happened to him in Sudan, the government put him in the ghost house, because he was just telling the public opinion about occurring behind closed doors in Sudan.

That type of expulsion was wired and indicates that there was a kind of collaboration between the two dictator regimes for exchanging such activists.

That type of expulsion made vast of Sudanese people fear of being activists in Cairo. The expulsion of Sushi also made me distrust all types of regimes and at the same time empowers me to look for another place where I can have my own freedom of expression and freedom of rights.

One evening, as I was walking about, I heard a Sudanese song that draws my attention! I stopped for a while to identify the direction and location. While I was stopping by the side of a nice building, a young man opened a small gate and came out. He looks Sudanese; he greeted me and asked if I wanted to join the party.

I said yes, actually I just stopped here to figure out the location of this party. I would love to join in. The young man guided me to the place and left. I went into the party hall and found a lot of people there. They were dancing, laughing; some of them were sitting listening to the song.

The singer was from Africa, the Sudan. His name is Wad Al Amen, he was singing a very nice song which describes the previous Sudanese revolution in October 1964. The songs tells us how Sudanese revolution at that time, took to the street across the cities in all the country claiming the military junta to step down and form an elected democratically government.

I sat by small table, next to me was an old man on a wheel chair. He was originally from Ethiopia, but lives in Cairo for more than 15 years. He was paying much attention to the song; I thought he knows the language very well. I did not interrupt him, after a while, he turned to me and asked about the name of the singer. I said I do not know the name.

We had a nice short conversation.

"Where are you from? I asked.

"I am originally from Ethiopia,"

How long have you been here? I inquired.

"I have been living in Cairo for more than 15 years,"

"How do you find Cairo," I investigated.

Cairo is the best city I liked in my life, adding that, he met many people from Africa particularly Sudan, most of them fled from Darfur in western Sudan. They fled from Sudan, because of the genocide in Darfur and Jebel Mara. He warned me to be careful while living here because he came to know that there were many Sudanese activists being deported to Sudan.

I responded to him that was incredibly sad. I enjoyed the party and I had learned that the majority of people in that party were Sudanese people who were conducting small business in Cairo.

As we were talking to each other, a young boy said dad we need to go home now. We said our goodbyes and they left.

The party was still continuing and many people were dancing. I went to the dancing-hall and danced for a while with some young people. There was a lot of food on tables. The party organizer announced ladies and gentlemen please feel free to help yourself our delicious food is waiting for you to try. I went to the dining-room and had delicious food and drink. I checked the time and it was already 4: am in the morning. But if you look around, you will see people walking by the side of roads, and cars, buses on the streets too, you sometime never know if that time was night or day.

Cairo is really a bewildering city. It looks busy all days a week. Many shops, stores and restaurants were opening 24 hours. As a tourist in Cairo you feel safe and thrilled while walking across the country. I do not know what Cairo is like nowadays, but it seems to be good with lots of possibility.

It was about five in the morning when I left the party. I was so glad to experience Cairo in its real life sight in the morning, afternoon and evening. I have learned from that night party Sudanese people were living in all parts of the world.

On one hand, Sudanese leaving their homeland for another land, their land would suffer and lack of employees and cheap labors. On the other hand, those Sudanese who left their land and live in the exile would learn different skills in different fields; someday they might return to their home and contribute with their knowledge in all walks of life.

Generally speaking, it is a permissible that people might explore over the Oceans, visit other places, see the sights and learn about the manners of other nation while visitation.

Sadly the Egyptians people have no rights to make a rally on the streets to express about their rights; they do not have permission to commit any kind of political activities in the name of any political body. There was only one party who was eligible for leading the country for no limit of time. That was how it works in many African countries; the abuse of human rights is still problematic in the country of Africa at large.

Adding to that, so many people left Cairo for Europe and never came back. Many others who decided to stay in that situation had become weak and never dare to speak out. That type of life style reminded me of where I fled from.

In the evening I saw the whole city decorated with different colors, red, yellow and green, I went to a big tent full of people and asked what was going on. "The great holy month of Ramadan is coming and all those signs you see, indicates love and peace." The preacher said.

I was so excited to be invited by the preacher and enjoyed the religious ceremony for the holy month of Ramadan. A lot of sweet, juice and dates piled on big tables for free.

The market was busy with people, some of them come shopping and others joining the crowd. I saw smile in their faces and sheer joy of receiving the great holy month of Ramadan. I saw old people sit in a circle which in Arabic is called "Halga". They knelt in supplication and request their Lord for forgiveness and mercy, most of them have a huge turban on their heads and chanting very humbly, at the same time, some other young people were in white performing a nice dance, some dancing slowly while others dancing quickly and spinning around.

That program reminded me of the same program that took place in my Island. That program functions as a gesture of welcoming holy Ramadan. But in the Island people do not dance and spin around, but they sit in a circle and knelt in supplication and ask their Lord forgiveness. They enjoyed celebrating the holy month and also trained their teenagers to try it for several days that type of training, assists their teenagers to have an idea about it and make them feel it into practice.

They feel hungry and thirsty while fasting and helps them to understand how much some other people in the corner of the world suffer from poverty. I used to fast someday while I was a little boy, it was hard for me in the beginning but later, I was used to it and now love it.

I had a camera at that time, I requested the organizer to take some photos but later, I left my camera in the Hotel and someone took it and I could not find it. I wish I had my camera back to show you the whole photos and the dances. I still remembered the whole photos that I took in Cairo, but they never returned to me a gain. They live in my memory. I remember all of them fondly.

I replay those moments in my mind &, I really would love to describe them to you to give you a sense of what I experienced.

I hope someday the person who took my camera from my living room in the Hotel would return it back to me. I wish I received them back, so I can show you all.

Chapter 4

FROM EGYPT TO INDIA (1992-2004)

I left Cairo for India in 1992 for educational goals. I did not know where to stay in India?

I did not know which university I go to? But I was very serious to get an offer of admission at a good university as soon as I arrived. The flight was very comfortable and the food was very good, so far better than the food I got back home.

In India, I went and looked for an offer of admission at some universities in the city of New Delhi before my visa expired. Fortunately, I got an offer of admission at the University in Udaipur city. The University of Udaipur helped me to get a student visa instead of a tourist visa. Within two weeks I got student visa and stayed legally at the city of Udaipur. I was happy to begin my new journey. I studied Bachelor of Arts in English; the duration of the program was three years. While I was studying at the university, I meet many students from the heart of Africa; I met with two hundred students from the same country where I came from.

I found out that students had a community center where they can meet at the end of the day. They also had different activities and that type of community made me thrilled. I was a new matriculate student at the college. I went to the community center for international students and presented a lecture entitled "The Significance of Learning English". That lecture drew the attention of all international students who belong to that community center to get to know my ability in speaking English. A year later, I was elected as a president for the community center.

In the final year, I worked as a volunteer for a year at Seva-Mandir organization.

Where there is sorrow, where there is poverty and oppression, where man is inhumane to man, and where there is the darkness of ignorance, it's there that SEVA-MANDIR is reaching out.

Seva-Mandir is a voluntary organization autonomous to the government, founded by Dr. Mohan Sinha Mehta in the year of 1968. The NGO works with tribal and other communities in Udaipur District mainly with six Blocks: KHERWARA, BADGAN, JHADOL, GIRWA, and KOTRA AND GOGUNDA.

Seva Mandir is one of India's leading development nonprofit organizations. Since 1968, Seva Mandir has partnered with 360,000 people across 700 villages of southern Rajasthan, one of the world's most impoverished places where people live on an average of $0.70 a day. Seva Mandir runs a comprehensive range of programs that ensure families have clean drinking water and can grow enough food to eat, offer disadvantaged students a quality primary education and non-formal education.

Seva-Mandir's present work includes a wide range of activities from adult literacy. Non-formal education for children, construction of community centers, major afforestation and women's development work to more technical activities like small scale irrigation projects. These activities are undertaken by the following resource units: Health, women and child care, wasteland development, people's management school, education unit, the folk culture and publication unit.

I graduated from the university within three years, in English literature and economics. After graduation, I joined the organization and worked as a volunteer in the education unit.

I had been volunteering for a year and wrote a project entitled: Field study on ways to increase peoples' participation in adult and non-formal education. During that time, I met with a lot of volunteers that came to the Organization from Africa, England, America and Canada. I also made a lot of friends from the western countries and attended a lot of workshops and seminars related to adult education and non-formal education.

I studied the historical background about Adult Education in the past by SEVA-MANDIR.

I learnt from the literature that was available at Seva-Mandir that Adult education has been mainly running in two BLOCKS of Udaipur District, JHADOL and KOTRA BLOCK. I stated that "I would like to focus on JHADOL BLOCK as a part taken to represent the whole. In JHADOL, SEVA-MANDIR has been working on Adult education since 1982.

In 1992, the new program of TLC (total literacy campaign). But in such program there were no literacy centers, but only door to door contacts, and teaching through volunteers. In that condition, the volunteer instructor works in the field and at the time teaches the adults in the house or in any other place. I studied and collected the materials from different sources. I held interviews with people from different villages in order to get broad view of their knowledge and needs. Then I put my reflection on proposed program of Seva- Mandir in Adult education:

- The main base of the program is that there should be education centers in the villages

- Running adult education center in each village is very important to cover all illiterates' people in the selected villages.

- To achieve total literacy I proposed that an entire family to be made literate by one volunteer from the same family.

- The volunteer instructor should be a local person who is motivated to serve the community.

- When there is a center it means that all the adult learners regularly meet together to chat and discuss problems and work out possible solutions.

- The volunteer instructor should be early trained before the opening of the centers in order to make the program most effective.

- I believe that it should be better to open the center in the instructor's house to ensure his attendance.
- Classes should start early in the afternoon so as to finish early in the evening and also to encourage the participation of women.

  Finally, I hoped that my suggestions would be approved and implemented by the people involved in the field of adult education.

I submitted my proposals and suggestions to Seva-Mandir Organization and moved to the capital of India for better life.

Luckily, I worked as a translator in different Arabian Embassies in New Delhi. I have been working as a translator in different Arabian Embassies in New Delhi for more than five years.

One such example, I worked as a translator at YEMEN EMBASSY in NEW-DELHI for years, my position was to read Indian newspapers everyday morning.

I remembered there were more than six Indian newspapers published simultaneously in English.

I just go through the headlines of the articles, if I find any article talks about the Middle East, I will translate it from English into Arabic.

I also participated in many seminars in the name of the Embassy; I used to receive invitation to deliver presentation about the relationship between the two countries.

I remembered one of the big events that I participated in, it was called Arab-India relationship.

In that event you have to deliver a topic related to the development of the relationship between the two countries.

For instance, one high level of delegation from Yemen visited India at that time and signed several agreements in the field of education, agriculture and information technology.

I translated that entire event from English into Arabic and submitted it to the Embassy, it was very unique experience, I made a lot of friends and learned a lot from them.

I sometimes meet Indian ministries in several meetings to discuss some issues related to business and how we can enhance the relationship between the two countries in several fields.

When I began my work as a translator for the first time at the Embassy, I did not know how to speak English well, but I studied and listened a lot and the result was very promising.

I believe my work at the Embassy in India allows me to learn good English and to understand what the Embassy does. To be honest, what I had learned in missions, I had never learned at Universities. However, that was not an invitation for students to leave universities and join missions.

I also have been working at Kuwait News Agency (KUNA) in New-Delhi for three months. I used to translate short stories from English into Arabic. It was very good experience.

I still remembered the head of the Agency. His name Khalid, he was very friendly, and kind to me, but for some reasons, I did not continue working for him. But I brought him an expert writer at that time. While I was working at the Embassies, from time to time, I delivered a lecture in the community center where the international student got together to raise awareness among them. I taught them about the dictator regime in our lovely land, how it abused the human rights. Owing to my political activities in New-Delhi, my name was posted as a black listed and wanted back home.

I started along with my colleagues a political movement. As an active member in that political movement, I delivered many lectures and had spoken in many symposiums to raise awareness among the international students studying in India as well as among the Indian people at large. Some of those speeches delivered in criticizing some of the military Junta ministries who used to visit India from time to time. I have been organizing many seminars, and the mission of my origin country in India and its supporting elements brought me under their focus.

I remembered the day when the majority of Sudanese students led a rally against the military regime in Sudan in front of Sudanese Embassy in India. The Embassy led a conspiracy and convinced the Indian government to arrest all of them including me for fifteen days.

We have been in prison waiting list room for more than fifteen days. The room size was bigger than the classroom. We were about 5o people that were kept in one room. We slept on the floor. We found ourselves as students amongst many other Indian prisoners who had committed actual crimes, most of them were older in age. Most of them had killed, stolen and did all sorts of bad things, but they were very nice to us. We told them that we have been arrested here because we organized a big rally in front of our Embassy claiming for demonstrating decency and justice in our home of Sudan. That is why we have been arrested. All of the prisoners laughed at us and told us that it was our right to do so, as long as you are in a democratic country.

They taught us during those days a lot of good and bad things that had happened to them in their life. Actually we learned from their life experience. They also told us to escape from the prison and they taught us that every Friday, the prison will be opened for visitors and at that period of time the security guard would be busy with many things we could leave one by one, if the gatekeeper asked just tell him that " We are visitor" and leave.

It was really very good idea and many of my friends who had a UNHCR certificate left the prison and nobody stopped them. I remembered one of our friends who looked exactly like Indian, kept on coming and going from time to time to the prison and spend much time with us and leave. He became very good friend to the security guard and convinced him that he would come from time to time see his friends.

Actually the idea behind that act all Sudanese students should be arrested and deported to Sudan for torture. But the mission and its supporting elements in India had failed to achieve that, because the UNHCR had intervened and stopped that plan from happening.

It was very hard to sleep on the floor in winter and we do not have any blanket or cover to rely on. But eventually the UNHCR approached the jail and released all of us. It was very difficult moment for students in their life but at the same time that event helped them to be more aware of conspiracies.

We lived in a country where that practiced democracy for many years and all Indian media criticize that event and pressure the Indian government to respect the values of human rights in terms of freedom of expression and freedom of rallies.

I experience with the military junta in the northern part of Africa taught me enough lessons in the trust and mistrust of the dictator with my fear of returning back to face the ghost house, the African mission in India leading all types of conspiracies against me, so I was forced to approach UNHCR Office in India for the necessary protection which has kindly offered to me.

I also remembered the Sudanese opposition movement in New Delhi. That body was very active and submitted a lot of press media to UNHCR to raise awareness among Sudanese students and Indians about the anarchist system in Sudan.

The leader of the Sudanese opposition movement in India was also played a vital role to inform the Indian government about the situation in Sudan. He added, if they had been deported to Sudan, they would have been tortured. They were also so many activists like him in New Delhi during that tenure.

I never gave up; I continued talking about the political situation in Sudan and what the regime had done to destroy to our land and people in different ways. The regime came to power in 1989 and ruling the land for more than 29 years. During this time, the situation was declining in every way.

I was lucky to get a decent job as a translator in different Embassies in India, through that position; I interacted with many ministers and V.I.P. who worked in different missions. I also learned and trained to be a good translator in seminars and conferences whenever it was required. That moment of time, helped me to build a good relationship with many employees in different Indian institutions.

Reflecting back home, I found out that the life style was the same. It had never changed. While staying in India, I decided not to give up hope and return home. I wanted to move forward to a better place than India. I stated "education is the only way that can help people to be aware of the significance of positive change in every walk of life".

From Canada to England (2000)

In the year 2000, I flew to Great Britain to do Master degree in Arts at the University of Durham. On the plane I begin talking to an English man, Mr. Johnson, who was sitting next to me.

Pardon me, how long does it take from Toronto to Manchester?

Johnson: Five hours, I assume. We can check it on this information book. Yes, that is right. We will be in Manchester city in half an hour

Are you a businessman?

Johnson: No, I am a University professor. Adding that, Are you a businessman?

Oh, no, I am a postgraduate student.

Johnson: that is interesting, Which University are you going to?

I am going to Durham University, How far is it from Manchester?

Johnson: Oh, about few miles. The train takes few hours, do not worry, I am going to Durham University too. I can help you if you have any obstacles.

I have a friend of mine studying there; he is going to meet me at Manchester airport. Anyhow, I can help you if you do not see your friend there.

I arrived at seven O'clock in the evening at Manchester airport, but I did not see my friend there. I was a little bit panic, when I could not see him at the airport. But Mr. Johnson said to me do not worry lets go through the customs exit.

I followed him and we managed to get through the customs exit quickly, but I did see my friend, he was not there.

Can I hire a taxi to Durham?

Johnson: You could, but it is very expensive. We better take the train. It is much cheaper. It goes faster too.

We went down stairs at the airport where there is a ticket-office.

We got our train-ticket from Manchester to Durham. I was so excited and thrilled to get a window seat, from there; I could be able to see the country side while the train was moving. It was summer time, and everything looks green and cool.

Professor Johnson told me that he works at the department of Education. He teaches Adult learners in Education. He has been working at Durham University for 7 years. He was so supportive and compassionate. He encouraged me after finishing my graduate study to get a Ph.D. in Education from Durham. I promised him to achieve my higher degree, but I did not know that it was very expensive to study in England.

I arrived at Durham University in the evening, but my old friend did not show up at the train station to take me to my accommodation. I took a taxi and went to University, when I arrived, I saw my old friend Aaron who had already spent 2 years there. I am very sorry I could not met you at the train station, Aaron apologized, But I was sick. I am much better now.

Aaron took me to my small room

Figure 4. A photo of my computer desk at Ustinov College, Durham city.U.K, September 25, 2011.

I arrived in Durham on 14 October. Wow! I was very impressed by Ustinov College community. I like my sweet room-it may be look small, but it has everything.

International students are very welcome here, and I have met many students here from different parts of the world.

Given my previous work in translating and interpreting between English and Arabic, which I have done for more than five years in Arab embassies in New Delhi, India, and my previous work as a volunteer for a year at the NGO Seva Mandir, a non- profit organization working with the rural population in the Udaipur District of Southern Rajasthan in India. I have consistently developed and maintained professional and friendly relationships with other people.

Figure 5. A photo of Ustinov Community college, Durham city.U.K, September 25, 2011.

On my first day at Durham, I keep on losing my way in the Ustinov community college, although a map guide in my hand was helping me a lot to find my way to classes.

It was one year study at Durham community, but it was full of joy and happiness around the university building. It was summer and the weather was very nice, this place looks so green and touching. I was looking at the rich green lawns around the Ustinov community college. It was sunny.

I made a lot of friends at the Ustinov Community college. The Ustinov Community college is very vibrant and moving. There I found different interesting activities. It is very easy to neglect your studies and spend much time playing games, watch movies or going for a walk, you have to be careful in time management.

I cannot tell you everything that I saw. Some students find accommodations in town. Each college has its own lodging, cafeteria, library and dining hall.

I settled-down at Ustinov community college. I started my classes in the mornings and some of them in the evenings, and then I realized that the cost of living in Durham is higher than the cost of living in Canada.

I looked for the part-time job to support myself. I was lucky at that time; I got a part-time job at a High School while doing my graduate studies. I managed to live and paid off my bills.

I made a lot of friends while I was studying at Durham University, and I still in touch with my previous friends. One of my previous friends at Durham University moved to Canada last year.

He came from South Africa to study public administration at Toronto University. He liked Toronto community and its cultural activities. He liked living here, but he does not like living by himself. He planned to bring his family here.

We talked together about our previous school days at Durham, but my friend says he prefers Canada to England in terms of standard of living. Adding that, the two countries are so great and nice but Canada is the best in every way.

I really agreed with him that we live in a diverse community where we see all ourselves equal in all rights of citizenship. That is why so many people from different countries would love to live forever in Canada.

I spent a year in England, but I had never got an opportunity to visit London. I visited some cities near Durham while I was living in Durham. I hope someday I get another big opportunity to revisit England as a tourist and spend some good time in London.

The only thing that I noticed during my stay in Durham, there was a lot of unemployment amongst the students. It was very difficult to get a job during that time. The city is small and it does have small scale industries and it was very overcrowded with national and international students.

I felt so happy that I live in Canada where I can navigate and get a job opportunity in more than one place, for instance, students in Canada have access to job in many sectors and the government also encouraged them to have at least part-time job to manage cost of living and gain some work experience.

After completing my graduate program I returned to Canada happily, but I notice the international crisis around the world has a negative impact on all economics in many countries at large. For example, here in Canada nowadays, the job opportunities is getting much more difficult for the Adults, but life is still much better than many other countries. The job markets become very competitive, where there are few jobs these days. The job environment is getting more corrosive each year.

North America

It was true there were so many sad stories and happy stories took place in North America. So many young people from Africa, and Asia left their mainland for Canada, because of oppression. They never wanted to go back, nor do they wish to remember their ugly past. In reality, it was and still is happening here for so many immigrants.

Some other immigrants have come to Canada and got a very decent job and supported their families back home. But that type of success required hard working in education and Canadian experience. For instance, there were so many Asian physicians moved in and worked in Canadian hospitals. They had already become Canadians in their way of living, culturally and socially.

One big family includes three daughters and two young boys who moved from Asia to Canada for a better life. They fled from their home because of the civil war. They moved to Alberta Canada.

The two young boys went to school for three years and quit. Their names were Hassan and Hussein. They were from a very conservative family. They learned to speak English fluently. They got full time jobs at Toyota. They do not understand the way of life.

They did not go to college or University to learn about Canadian culture. They did not believe in co-education when boys and girls study together in one classroom based on their own cultural background.

They thought with their own way of life and act accordingly. Their father was old and did not pay attention to his two young boys. One evening Hassan was in his car at the parking lot waiting for his younger brother to come from work. While he was waiting there, a group of young people approached him and told him that "if you want to make easy money please join us,"

Hassan did not understand what they were talking about. The young group left him alone, but some of them told him "no worries' we will chat again. After a while, his young brother arrived and both of them went to the restaurant to have lunch. They usually spent most of their time together. They had a plan and began to work on it.

A week later, one gentle man came to Hassan home and knocked on the door. It was on weekend. Hassan came out and opened the door. The gentle man greeted him and told him that he would like to talk to him in person. Hassan left the house and both of them went to the corner of the house and the gentleman said to Hassan, "I want you to work with us. We are drug dealers, we made a lot of money, I promised you within few months you will change your life financially." It very simple, I would give you the drug and sell it to people and I would show you how to do it. Hassan was a kind of hesitant at first, but the gentleman put his hand in his

pocket and gave five hundred for just a commission.

The gentle man told him never ever tell anyone that you know me we should do this type of business undercover once it was no legally allowed. Hassan did not tell his brother that he was going to do that work. He started doing the business for several months and made a lot of money and even his brother was shocked how Hassan made that money in several months?

He bought a new car and introduced a lot of new things in the house such as furniture. He eventually told his youngest brother about the work and both of them engaged in it.

After one year, they bought a new house and moved in from their apartment. They decided to leave the work because they made a lot of money. They made sufficient money to start their own business in down-town, the gentleman told them if you quit from the job that means the end of your life.

One day on weekends, while they were sitting in their back yard of the new house. One member of the drug dealers came slowly in his hand a loaded pistol and shot them at short range and left. Their neighbors heard the gun shot and called the RCMP.

The police within no time presented and took the causalities to hospital. They had already been dead at the scene. That was the sad ending of that family who came to the land of opportunities and dreams. Their parents were very sad indeed and live all their rest of life in sorrow.

Three girls their names were Ana, Mona and Lila. They were very smart at school. They did very well at high school in their final exam. In the end of the semester, they were very glad at having received good marks in their final exam. They all entered the college to study nursing. The three girls have managed to graduate from the college and work full-time job in the hospital to take care of their parents.

On the other hand, one small young boy had come from the Refugees camp in Asia to Canada in 2000. His age was 22 years old. The rest of his family had been killed in the civil war back home. He did not have any relative or siblings in Canada to take care of him? He got loan from the government and went to school, sadly he met some bad groups and hang around with them for a while as friends. He started smoking marijuana and becomes most of his time intoxicated. He stops going to school. He turns into a burglar. He attempted many times to break through houses and shops. He had been in prison for many times and released.

The marijuana was becoming available and accessible to young boys around the corner. The type of accessibility helps many young boys to be addicted to it. It was really dangerous for a young boy to live in a free country and transgress the boundaries of freedom. He enjoys life by doing all sorts of bad temptations, and he does not understand that he abuses the space of freedom. Of course, the role of his parents was absent and that gap helps him in the name of freedom to do what he wants. Eventually he was trying to break the ATM and the security guard caught him and put him in prison.

This is one of the unique story that I heard while living in Canada, a couple of years, I met a gentleman originally from Ethiopia, but lives and works in Kitchener, his name is Adam. I actually met him at the Tim Horton's as I was sipping some tea.

The gentleman was from Ads Abba the capital of Ethiopia. He has been living in Kitchener for more than ten years. He told me that there was once a big family composed of five members, a father, a mother and two daughters and a big son came to Canada as a refugee through UNHCR.

The whole members of the family do not speak English at all. They arrived at Toronto International airport. The coordinator who supposed to receive them at the airport does not show up during their arrival. They arrived in the evening. The coordinator does not know that the family will be at the airport in the evening. He received a call from the head office of UNHCR in Ethiopia that the flight has been cancelled and the family will be arriving in Toronto next day morning.

In fact that call was not accurate and the family had arrived in the evening on time by Etihad airways. But no one received them and do not know English to tell their story. Luckily, there was one gentleman who works at the airport and knows their dialect. He communicated with them and got to know that they were coming from Ethiopia and someone should receive them here. He went and informed the manager of the airport about that family, from their documents the manager understood they were refugees, he took them by his own car to a hotel and let them to have a rest and went to find out.

Next morning the coordinator at the airport inquiring about their arrival but they told him that the family had already arrived last night, and the manager of the airport took care of them. The coordinator met the manger and thanked him for all his generosity and took them in a big car to their destination which was small community where the population not more than two hundred.

All the community were waiting for the family, they received the family with warm hospitality and big party in the evening all the community members were there. The new family was very impressed and amazed by the great party. But they do not know to speak a simple sentence to the people.

and I love you," this phrase stuck in the boy 'mind even though he does not understand English, but he just assumes it was a nice expression. During that night party there were a lot of food and cakes, one old lady was in a wheel chair wanted to eat some cakes but her son for some reasons refused to let her taking some cakes.

An older boy who has just arrived from Ethiopia was noticed that the lady needed the cake but her son refused. He immediately took his plate which was full of cakes and handed it to her. The lady says "thank you my favorite son.

The new family lives for several months within that community, but the father told his son to find a place where they can interact with some people who know their language. Eventually, the family moved to Calgary and lived there. While they were living there, the young boy within three years learned to speak and understand English very well.

The young boy now knows English and remembered the quote from the old lady when he was a new in Canada, he cries and says to himself, I would like to revisit that place and say thank you again for all the community helpers. He went by himself to the village and met with all people. They received him with hospitality and each one wanted to invite him home for food or tea.

At the same time, he revisited the lady on the wheeled-chair and she immediately recognized him and started crying and hugging him.

Why did you leave us my son?

And the boy also started crying too.

I recalled this story, because it tells us about the generosity of Canadians in terms of supporting the new Canadians upon their arrival to Canada.

I am in the habit of reading the newspaper "Waterloo Region Record". I feel uneasy if I do not read the newspaper titled the Record.com. I spend half an hour in the morning and an hour in the evening to cover all the headlines in the record. The record talks about the city news, current jobs postings in the Kitchener region.

I very much excited that things have worked out so well for me and got a job at the University at the department of languages and literatures. In the first day at work, Professor James showed me the schedule and the classroom where I work with my students. Next day, 1 was so excited to see someone delivering the newspaper to our department every day morning. I feel uneasy if I do not read the newspaper in the morning. I liked the university building and small classrooms that composed of 25 students.

Sunday morning, I received the newspaper in my office, but I do not have time on that day to look at it in the morning. I went to class and came back to my office, I remembered I had a good time and long break, because of the midterm exam, I took the newspaper and started reading the headlines, I suddenly came across a headline says Sudanese protesters took across the street in all cities and towns in Sudan. I was so surprised and astonished to see that report in the Canadian newspaper about the Sudan. I read it and understood that in the beginning of December,2019 thousands of Sudanese protesters took to the streets in all cities of Sudan, demanding the Dictator Omer Al-Bashir to step down from power, but the government forces responded to the protesters with excessive force. Despite rumors that the government would use live bullets to disperse protesters, they remain in their stand and peaceful revolution that has beautiful slogans:

- Freedom
- Peace
- Justice

Sudanese protesters whose months of protests prompted the ouster of Omar Al-Bashir, Sudan's president for thirty years, on April, 2019, and the new establishment of a transitional government in Sudan created an opportunity to restore long term suability.

The December revolution paid off the price and lost large number of protesters, but the new government in power now is working hard to find the perpetrators and to bring them to justice.

It will take time for the new government to rebuild Sudan to respects all types of human rights. All Sudanese around the globe would collaborate with new government to restore peace, freedom and justice in Sudan.

Recently the Prime Minister of the transitional government in Sudan Dr. Hamdok and the president of

France Macron at joint conference, **Macron** *"commended the Sudanese revolution and described it as similar to France Revolution in terms of demands. He lauded the Sudanese youth courage in resisting the ousted regime and achieving victory for the Sudanese will.*

President Macron adding that *"the Sudanese December revolution will pose a source of inspiration to the entire world, indicating that his admiration of the Sudanese revolution has motivated his to speak about it before the recent UN General Assembly's 74th session.*

The change in Sudan made me so optimistic to think seriously of finding a new way of helping people in Sudan.

The best thing I could do in helping Sudanese people is to form a non-governmental organization in the field of education and to work in the rural areas in Sudan to raise awareness among people about the importance of democracy.

I still see the situation in Sudan is fragile but it is on the right track and all Sudanese supported it and work to improve it for better. A week later, all the news nationally and internationally started talking about the Sudanese revolution, it becomes an excellent example for many nations around the globe.

The protesters never use violence, it was very peaceful revolution and all Sudanese people participated in it in different peaceful ways, nationally and internationally.

Someday Professor James invites me for coffee at Tim Horton. We sat by the tea-table talking about the new professor who has just joined the department of Engineering. His name is Professor Mike.

The next morning, Professor Mike was invited to breakfast by the department of languages and was introduced to the staff of languages and literatures.

"This is a welcome treat!" I exclaimed, looking at the supply food on the table. In time I have been thinking a lot about the letter which I received from the person whom I do not remember. The letter makes me think much about it from time to time.

I ask Mike about his previous work experience. Professor Mike says he has been working in Germany for three years contract to design a new map project that shows the town of Giessen. I immediately interrupted him and exclaim! Giessen! But you know, actually a week ago, I got a letter from Germany sent by an Engineer his name is Wolf Müller. I do not remember that I have such a friend. I every day try to remember and I do not remember him at all, my earliest memory does not help me.

Wow! Wow! Wolf Muller, he is the head of the new map project that shows the town of Giessen," Mike said. I know this man very well; he is my best friend and he was the head of my map project. I still have his phone number and e-mail address. But I did not contact him since I left Germany for a while.

"I can talk to him if you like and let you as soon as possible," Mike said

Mike rang up Wolf Muller and left him a short message on his voice mail to get back to him as soon as possible. He also sends him a message in his email saying I am so sorry sir to bother you now, but it seems to be important.

I look forward to hearing from Mike about Wolf Muller!

Book 11

There was uneasy long journey that begins from far and wide to the small Island. It was an expected visitor to the Island on the River Nile. The visitor who came from far and wide was looking for his old friend.

The visitor came from Germany. He had a lot to tell his friend in the Island. He had something to do with his old friend in the Island. He was so optimistic to meet with his old friend in the Island.

He had a message to achieve in meeting with his old friend in the Island. He was so confident that his friend was waiting for him to surprise him in the Island.

His visit to the Island might raise many interesting points. Why does the visitor care so much to visit the heart of Africa, the small Island?

Readers have the write to investigate and raise questions about the significant of the visitor.

Tomorrow readers will come to know the importance of the visit and how does it work? And why?

Why does the visitor care? Why does the visitor want to change his friend life? These questions help readers to understand that the visitor is a community helper and creative problem solver in a community at large.

The visitor has so many connections in and out his country in terms of social development and education learning program.

The visitor was hoping to make his old friend succeed in his career by supporting him to come to Germany; in this regard, the visitor stood on his feet and travelled to the heart of Africa, with full of hope and inspiration.

The visitor believes in strive for change.

Strive for getting what you want and deserve

Strive for gaining knowledge and acknowledge
Strive for studying what you interested in it
Strive do not be surprise!

Strive for better is always something good to do in our lives. In particular, strive for education is a core point in each person who looks to get an open window to go through. Belfour is one of many adventurers who strive for positive change in his career.

He built a strong relationship with the western countries while he was student at high school. He built a friendship and understanding with Muller while touring the Sudan in Kosti town. That type of friendship last for long and opened doors to Belfour to understand the importance of exploring to other countries and learn something new.

On the other hand, Muller was in touch with Sudan since his first trip in the ninety. The picture of Sudan and its people was always in Muller eyes. Muller from time to time, would love to reconnect himself with Belfour. He could not find any other better way to connect himself with Africa than revisiting Sudan.

Muller wanted to meet again with Belfour in Africa. Muller wanted to reward Belfour for his kindness and generosity. He wanted to send him to Germany to study there. He wanted to offer Belfour a new space of learning environment.

Muller did not know that Belfour had already left Sudan for somewhere. He liked to see his old friend after such a long time. He started his long journey for the island which is on the river Nile.

Chapter 5

REVISIT THE HEART
OF AFRICA

IN THE THIRTY YEARS THAT HAVE PASSED, the professor Muller became the head department of the Engineering Section at Giessen University in Germany. He thought that, he would do something to help his friend Belfour whom he met in the Heart of Africa long time ago.

He revisited the Sudan and went to Kosti town on the river Nile to remember the place and the Sudanese food he liked which was "porridge". Back in 1989, Muller was having "porridge" with a student Belfour and some thing he said has stuck with his up to this time. He went to the same lodging that he used before.

But there was no lodging anymore in the city. There were new hotels in different life styles and they were very expensive. He spent one night at one of the beautiful hotels in the city. He went to the market in the city looking for his favorite food which was "porridge" it was made of wheat and water very traditional food. Unfortunately, he did not find it, he was very sad in deed. He decided to look for "porridge" in the Island where Belfour used to live.

Next morning, he went to Kosti harbor looking for the ferry that used to connect people between the two cities, Kositi and Aljazeera. Fortunately, the ferry was still there, he went and asked someone was waiting for the ferry to go to the Island "Aljazeera"

The person who was waiting for the ferry used to work as a ticket collector in the ferry, but now he was retired. He was a kind man, he looked old but very strong. He spoke English very well. He had been to England for a while and he knew English very well. Professor Muller was impressed by his language abilities and kept asking him about the ferry.

How many times the ferry crosses the river" Muller said.

"The ferry crosses the river three times a day,"

"May I ask you some questions?" The man said.

"I would be more than happy to answer you," Muller said.

"Where are you from," the man said.

"I am from Germany, Giessen city," Muller said.

"Are you a tourist," The man said.

"I just revisited the Island which I was here before thirty years ago. Muller said.

"Oh the ferry is here, you can get your ticket inside the ferry it is only 20 dinars," The man said.

"It was nice social chat, have a good day, I hope we meet again before going to Germany," Muller said.

Muller sat in the end of the ferry watched waves rolling behind waves. It took half an hour to reach the opposite side of the river Nile. While the ferry was sailing on the river Nile, Muller was enjoying the fresh air and taking photos of the river shore.

He got off the ferry and went to see the same garden he had seen before. But there was no garden, all trees were withered and died. He took a taxi to the down town. He found a lot of things had changed. The city was growing and some people moved in and some people moved out.

The good thing was, he met so many new people who could be able to communicate with him in simple English. He talked to people in town and asked about Belfour, but no one knew Belfour. He went to the high school but he found a different high school in a different place and knew teachers, he does not know them. He kept talking to people about his main visit to meet with his old friend was student at the high school long time ago.

He spent three days in the city searching for his friend but he did find any information which led to him. He actually wanted to help empower more students from the heart of Africa to become corporate scholars in Africa. For the last moment, while he was leaving the island, he met with teacher Altyab, he was a history teacher at the old high school. He told Muller, he used to work at the old high school a long time ago. Adding that "the student Belfour left the island before thirty years ago and never come back, and even never write anymore,"

In the Island Muller being invited by one of Belfour friend to small restaurant to attempt porridge, he ate porridge and drank a tea with milk. While Muller was eating porridge his stomach was upset and stopped eating it. He felt immediately with stomach ache and starting vomiting.

He said to himself this porridge was totally different from the previous one that I had at Belfour home. I do not know the ingredients and also while I was eating it, I noticed all dishes in the restaurant were dirty and he came to know that it was the matter of hygiene.

He went immediately to the hospital in the town and the Doctor told him that you should not eat food outside and particularly in such small restaurant. If you would like to eat food you should to go to specific restaurants in town that present good services

"I have been invited by one villager in the town," Muller said.

"Please take two pills per day, and never eat food again in small restaurants," the Doctor instructed. Adding that, there were a lot of changes took place in the Island, For instance, the food in down-town was always getting worse and worse and the drinking water was not clean too.

In the meantime, the Doctor invited Muller for dinner-table at his home. Firstly the Doctor asked him if he is vegetarian or non-vegetarian!

"I am non-vegetarian," Muller responded.

Next day, indeed, Muller went to the Doctor's residence for Dinner-table. It was very neat and tidy. He met him with several Doctors who work in the Hospitals. Some of them have been graduated from England and some of them have been graduated from the United States. Most of them have abroad and knows English very well.

Muller spent a very good time with the Hospital-staff and came to know that Sudanese are so great and kind in every way, and he also believed that they are so educated and smart in their fields.

At the end of the meal, Muller thanked all the hospital staff for their kindness and left Island with two different impressions, the first good impression he met with ordinary people and educators in the Island, and that type of social interaction made him to learn about Sudanese culture.

The bad impression, Muller was very much disappointed and deeply saddened, because he did not meet with his old friend Belfour to make him a gentleman.

He came to town intentionally to take Belfour with him to Germany to study there; but he did not meet with Belfour. He had been informed that Belfour had already left Sudan for somewhere.

Muller decided to look for other options to help the communities in different places that are currently in need of help. He visited many countries in Africa and Asia to see how they look like, and at the same time, he went there to support those poor families are in need of supportive in the field of education

Muller left the island for Germany very sadly; he decided to support the international students from Africa to study in Germany. He connected his department with many Universities in Africa to accept some students for some technical programs in Engineering and waste land development. He assisted many students from Africa and Asia particularly India.

There was a non-governmental organization in Udaipur city, India runs a huge project in Education and waste land development, through the department of Engineering with the help of its head department Professor Muller does a lot small projects in the rural area around the city Udaipur.

Professor Muller visited the Organization himself and delivered several proposals related to the waste land development. He also made a lot of friends and students from the poor family background to help.

Professor Muller said in his statement "the only problem for the new students from Africa and Asia in Germany, they have to learn the German language before starting their programs," adding that all of the international students are young and ambitious to learn the language and I assume that they are smart enough to grasp the German language in short terms.

He has been fortunate working with different international students around the globe as they contend with how to motivate local student in their countries participating in a growing communities.

He gave several examples for some international students who came to study at Giessen University and they do not have any German background. They studied the language and now most of them are working in different projects in the country.

One such example, I had a student from the heart of Africa his name is Adam; he came from Jebel Marra in the western Sudan. He came here in 1990. He didn't know the German language, he is now a member of our staff at the department of engineering, he is a professor now, he teaches technical engineering, and so many like him across the country.

I know that there are so many smart students in Africa, if they get opportunities in the western countries, they would become a part of many positive changes across the globe. That is why I liked to do as much as I can to support them. "I considered the whole world as one body, if one part does not function well; it will impact negatively on the whole body.

THE GOOD NEWS, last year Professor Adam revisited Jebel Marra in Sudan and helped his people in the mountain to utilize the water and supported them to work on the waste land development in different hilly area in the western Sudan. He made a huge fundraiser along with some nonprofit organization to help mobilize schools for children two.

We sent some tents to some people in Africa, because sometimes the heavily rain washed away many houses and they have no shelter to live temporarily, we kept working with other organizations in Africa first is to identify the prioritized places and then we send our suppliers to reach out

Chapter 6

The information technology helps us to travel from country to country within short period of time. How that does happen? It does happen today when we fly by planes from west to west and from East to East within few hours.

We benefited from the information technology to send messages within seconds from country to country. We use technology to make our life much easier. How do we make our life much easier today?

We use technology in every way to live better life. In particular, at homes we use electricity to run all our small machines at homes and light all our rooms and kitchen to maintain our food in fridge from getting rotten.

The reason behind all these benefits, the story of this book it was something seems to be unbelievable, but now it is becoming believable and reflects the real life situation of many adventurer like Belfour who strive for better live.

Unbelievable story becomes believable!

The journey of Belfour functions as a connection between the West and Africa. The journey helps Belfour to understand the similarities and differences between one culture and another. The journey helps Belfour to get benefited from the whole places that he had been to.

Belfour becomes as a mission of navigator who navigates to gain knowledge and convey it to his people back home. Belfour learned and plan to learn his people in Africa about education and civilization in terms of standard of living. Belfour journey would be a pattern and unique example for the coming generation in Africa to strive and never be surprised!

Belfour's journey assist shaped his life and at the same time fascinated others who think in the same way. Belfour' journey motivated youth to work for change and leave no stone uncovered.

Unbelievable

The Waterloo city has become internationally known, because there are so many international students who study here. The university community becomes very vibrant and moving. In the meantime, some other universities would interest in collaborating with diverse program at Waterloo. However, different programs at different departments at Waterloo hosted international speaker in controversial issue that concerns the international public opinions. One such example, the current issue nationally is global warming.

The department of Engineering at Waterloo hosted a guest speaker from the department of engineering at Giessen University, Germany; to talk about "the disadvantages of information technology" The main speaker was Professor Wolf Muller, the head department of engineering at Giessen University, Germany.

At that time, many articles talked about this issue and it became the topic of the time in many places, so many people mislead the others by this technology, we need to find a proper way to protect our system form fraud and hackers. The main organizer at the department of engineering was my friend professor Mike who has recently become the head department of the engineering.

It was winter time, the forecast was mild, the symposium started at 7:00 PM and ended at 9:00 PM. I came a little bit earlier to the conference hall, but it was very full of audience. I sat in the first row with my friend

Mike who introduced the speaker. The speaker has a rich resume and he came to the stage and says Hello in German and then he translated it into English.

That moment made me to go back to my youngest days when I was a little boy, how old would I have been at that time, I could not remember exactly, but the speaker had drawn my attention to the past. While he was talking about the disadvantages of the information technology, I gazed at him and thinking about his character.

I asked myself if I met this man in my life before. I enjoyed his speech. He spoke very well in English. He talked more than an hour about his topic and then opened opportunities to audience for placing questions. It was the most successful symposium I had ever attended.

In a world where rapid information, and technology connect our cities, towns and villages are benefiting from it, we need a new sort of protected system to avoid disadvantage uses.

He says at the end of the symposium, he would love to work here and live in Canada, because the interest in learning about such a topic is very high and promising. He thanked all the organizers and audience for giving their time and knowledge to discuss this important issue.

At the end of the symposium we all went to the dining room to have some food and snacks. Everyone was very impressed by his new perspectives in terms of avoiding the disadvantages in our system. He also distributed his new article free of charge to all participants. His article talked about the same topic in brief. It was precise and concise.

I was very amazed by his charisma and personality, I got an opportunity to sit together by small table and have a social chat. Professor Mike was joining us and we all started sharing ideas, Professor Mike accepted Wolf Muller invitation as a main speaker at Giessen University for the next year in summer, but the topic was not yet decided.

Some audience came and asked the speaker about the same topic and I immediately left him to talk to them, we may continue in our social chat later if we had enough time. And also it depends on the speakers time and ability. He came from a long flight right to the conference room, he needed some rest too. I said to myself.

I went to the other side of the dining room and talked to some people who come from different places near waterloo city to attend the symposium. They also liked the topic and the way professor Muller presented it in detail. They would love to see more symposiums in such area of interest. I appreciated their feedback and proposals to the department of engineering. I promised to take all their proposals into our considerations and implement them accordingly.

While I was speaking with them, Professor Mike came and I introduced him to them as the head department of engineering and I left to find Professor Muller to resume our social chat. But he was still busy with some other audience who were impressed by his topic and the way he presented it.

I was shocked that the conference room was so full and even some audience was standing the number was more than the capacity of the room. I was waiting for a while to see if Professor Muller becomes free. And finally all the audience evacuated the conference room and we remained only Professor Mike, Professor Muller and I.

Professor Muller said he was a little bit tired and he needed to sit by the table for a while. While we were sitting by the table, he told us that he had been to the heart of Africa a long time ago, he visited the different places in Sudan and he was impressed by the generosity of Sudanese people.

He went further and said he went there intentionally to learn about Africa. He visited Small Island titled Aljazeera where on the river Nile, it was full of gardens and trees. It was really a thick garden in the heart of Sudan.

He revisited the same place before twenty years ago to meet with his previous friend in the island. He did not find him and everything was changed for worse and worse. The majority of trees and gardens were withered and died. He spent three days in the island kept asking people to help him find his previous friend.

While he was talking professor Mike interrupted him by saying why did you care a lot of him.

"He was very smart student and very ambitions to educate himself and become a gentle man," Muller said.

My plan was to meet him and help him to study in my country; recently I help many international students to study in Giessen University. Most of them were very successful in their programs.

"Do you know the name of the student whom you were looking for," I spoke.

"If I could remember, his name was David Belfour," Muller said. Adding that I sent him a letter if I could remember some parts of it, I remembered he was asking me about the universities in Germany and the admission procedures,"

I still remember this "what kind of information do you like about universities? There are a lot of them in Germany, maybe fifty; I think there is one in Giessen too. I got about 20000 students

Here," I invited him to visit my home in Kitchener before he catches an early Bus to Toronto International Airport and flies to Germany.

He was very pleased to visit my home but he does not have time to do so. His flight was the next day morning. We talked to the airways if they can reschedule it for the next day evening; fortunately, they accepted his suggestion and his flight have been rescheduled for the next day evening.

Next morning, I picked him up from Delta hotel to my home and offered him his favorite Sudanese food which was "porridge" was so thrilled to eat this porridge here in Canada and the taste of it took him back to his earliest memory when he was having it in Sudan. He says this taste of porridge was typically taste with the ones that I had in Sudan before twenty years ago.

I just said the hand maker for both of them in Sudan and Canada was one hand maker. Muller was shocked and said how do you know that porridge is my favorite Sudanese food?

And from whom you learn to make it?

He kept asking me many questions one after another

Where are you originally from?

I told him in brief how and why and when did I left my homeland for the last time and how much I suffered in my journey until I arrived in Canada. He was listening to me with pleasure in order to learn more about my personal story, but I did not start with my original place in Sudan while I was narrating my personal story.

I kept telling him about my personal experience while I was in India, Libya, Egypt and eventually he stopped me and said I really confused and please put me in the right track if I am wrong.

"Please eat first and then we can talk about all these issues while sipping our tea," I suggested.

"He was eating up all the porridge and asked me do you have some more,"

I made him the same porridge that my mom made in Sudan before and the same soup that he liked,"

"Thank you very much for this delicious porridge and now let us talk business," Muller thankful.

I brought the tea and coffee on the tea-table and asked him what you would like to drink,"

"He took tea and small piece of cake, and started talking about African people and how much he loves Africa. In particular, Sudan, I told him by the way I am from the heart of Africa from the Sudan.

He says what?

I said I am from the river Nile, the Sudan.

"I will tell one important thing that happened to me in my life, I have been to Sudan more than once, and I liked it and its people.

I said to him that was a good story for you and me in our life, just a minute let me show something, I will be right back to you.

I went to my bed room and brought an old album that includes a lot of pictures about different things in Canada and Africa and I moved his picture at the end of the album along with his written letter that I had received from him while I was in Sudan.

Muller started turning the pages of the album over and over; suddenly he came across his photo and the letter he wrote it to me before 20 years ago.

He stood up and exclaimed! Wow!

It was unbelievable you are a person whom I looking for

It was unbelievable story that becomes true
It was unbelievable story that becomes real
The person whom you looked it is I!
I am enclosing a few photos to give you an idea

Glossary

Tyba Garden: is a very big garden full of all types of fruits on the island on the river Nile.

Jalo-City. a Libyan place located on the border of Southern Region of Libya?

Brotha: slang language in African language which means brother in English.

Tripoli city: the capital of Libya

Stone: the Stone in this story means the hope and dream that you have to achieve

Macaroni: a kind of Libyan food that made of floor.

Azan: a person who calls people for prayers in the Mosque

Opera hotel: an old hotel in the city of Cairo.

Delhi: the capital city of India

Cairo: the capital of Egypt.

Falafel: one of the best Mediterranean food

Foul: a kind of beans that very famous in Egypt and Sudan

Alexandria: one of the biggest cities in Egypt, it is located on the Mediterranean sea

Jebel Mara: one of the biggest mountains in the western Sudan

Ramadan: the holy month of Muslims community

Halga: an Arabic word which means "circle" in English

Porridge: Traditional Sudanese food made by boiling flour in water

Activities

AFTER READING

Do you think that Belfour' life in different places admire you?

What did you learn from this book?

Would you recommend this book for adults to read?

Which of these places do you think you are going to visit about in the book? Why? Choose one of the following places:

- Canada
- England

- India
- Egypt
- Africa-Sudan.

How was Belfour different from other African students?

If you were in Belfour position, would you explore the globe?

Which books would you prefer to read?

- Novels
- Stories
- fictions

Belfour composed the following stanza and kept repeating it all time:

Do not be weak, you've reached the peak

Do not be weak, walk around the creek

Do not be weak, you deserve a treat.

Do not be weak, now sit on the peak

That kind of short trip in Tayba garden helps to attract students from other villages near the Island also to come to study at the high school. That type of social interaction was very moving and touching.

As I put the letter back in the envelope, I sat by the dinner-table trying to recall the past, the past that created my earliest memory

Printed in the United States
By Bookmasters